Art Textiles of the World

KOREA

TELOS

Editor: Mi-Kyoung Lee

Graphic Designer & Copy Editor: Matt Koumis

Assistant Designer and Typesetter: Jo-chieh Yao

Reprographics: Typoplus, Frangart, Italy

Printed in Italy

© Telos Art Publishing 2005

Brighton Media Centre

15 Middle Street

Brighton

BN1 1AL

England

editorial@telos.net

www.arttextiles.com

First printed December 2005, Italy

ISBN 1 902015 07 X

A CIP catalogue record for this book is available from the British Library

Note:

Biographies have been edited to a consistent length and are selections only.

Photo credits

Ja-Ryong Cho, Young-Guk Chun, Kyung-Yeun Chung, Jaeil Studio, Hyun-Ho Kim, Hyun-Woong Kim, Jeun-Soo Kwan, Man-Gyu Lee, Man-Hong Lee, Nemo Production, In-Gyu Oh, Kwang-Choon Park, Min-Ho Song, Hatakeyama Takashi.

The poem *Meditative Space* on page 3 is taken from *Esprit of Bojagi* p. 26, edited by Dong-Kwang Chang, publ. The Korean Culture & Art Foundation, 2002.

Editor's Acknowledgments

This book has come into being through contributions from many insightful eyes, hands, minds, and hearts.

I would firstly like to thank The Lindback Foundation for giving me the great opportunity to research contemporary Korean textile art in 2004. During my five-week visit to Korea, I met with 37 leading artists, educators, curators, and critics across the country. This book would not have been possible without the passionate work of these leaders in the field of textiles.

I would like to thank the ten featured artists in this book for their beautiful body of work, professionalism, and for their visions for the future of Korean textile art. The logistics of my intensive visits to Korea were facilitated by the tireless help and guidance of my dear friend and artist Hyuk Kwon. Thanks are due also to my brother Young-Joo Lee, who shipped me nearly a hundred books to the United States and was my cheerful driver through Busan. Prof. Kyung-Yeun Chung, Prof. Sung-Soon Lee, Prof. Soo-Chul Park, and Prof. Burn-Soo Song, have all been very generous with their opinions and information in support of this book. Discussions with critics Sun-Hak Kang, Dong-Kwang Chang, and Jae-Eun Lee and their works have had a significant influence on my writing.

I would also like to thank Gerhardt Knodel, Director of Cranbrook Academy of Art and Warren Seelig, Distinguished Professor at The University of the Arts, who have both shared their insightful points of view on the philosophies underlying current issues in the contemporary scene. Thanks too to Scott Klinker, Designer-in-Residence and Head of 3D Design at Cranbrook Academy of Art, for his support of my research and his helpful guidance.

Matt Koumis, director of Telos Art Publishing, helped me focus this research. His vision and philosophy on textile art has further inspired my own love of this field, which I've tried to capture on every page of this book. Thanks go also to the Telos team in England and Italy including Jo-chieh Yao, Natalie Davis, Josef Obkircher, Simone, and Ermanno Beverari.

Many of my assistants are current students and alumni of The University of the Arts in Philadelphia: Jae-Yu Lee, Siobhan Kiley, Elizabeth Doherty, Jennifer Gin, Byoung-Kwon Min, Jillian Hoover, and Christine Domanic have assisted and touched all steps of this publication process. My deep appreciation goes out to faculty and friends of The University of the Arts for their warm support and interest in this project.

Finally I would like to express my love and appreciation to my dear friends and family, especially to my parents Moo-Jin Lee and Moon-Yeam Kim to whom I dedicate this book in gratitude for their continuous love and encouragement.

Mi-Kyoung Lee

Indigo blue sky, you are our mirror

Seeds fly in the air

they germinate with vitality from the ground like green leaves

The four seasons with their varied hues

I bathe in each one of them

As I grow in mud, tears, and everyday life.

CONTENTS

Seasons arrive and fade away with the passing of time

The sounds of the birds, water and wind

And the everlasting Buddhist chants

Small scrap of the indigo sky

Glimpsed in the river, mountains and valleys

All things gradually regain their own colour

Meditative Space

by Dong-Kwang Chang

Chief Curator, Seoul National University

Museum of Contemporary Art

Sung-Soon Lee

The Land We Must Preserve

INTRODUCTION

In this introduction, I speculate about the connections between Koreans and cloth through historical, sociological, and psychological references. All ten artists who are featured within these pages conduct their own exploration of the meaning, tactility, and philosophy of cloth. Artists draw, paint, and sculpt with cloth or on cloth; manifesting the characteristics of cloth, and celebrating with flourishes of cloth. Their whole lives have been centered around cloth, which has become a symbol of Korean history and culture.

Koreans know nature. It is the essence of traditional Korean beauty; a fundamental part of our traditional culture, art, crafts, design, architecture, and textiles. Natural dyes of persimmon, and natural materials such as ramie or mulberry paper, are key ingredients in traditional arts and crafts processes. And natural materials and processes make up the surfaces of everyday life in Korea: for centuries dried rice straw has been used to make egg cartons, baskets, shoes, hats, rugs, hardware, walls, even roofs. The spirit, practice and economy of recycling have been essential to Korean life, long before any discussions of sustainability arose. The traditional textile *Jogakbo* was made up of small scraps of cloth remnants from the Period of the Choson Dynasty. Nothing went to waste.

Korea has a very dense population for such a small land. The traditional house was built for four seasons; its structure was low to the ground; rooms were small, with no storage. Textiles were brought into play, providing the main resource for room dividers, furnishings, multi-functional household objects, as well as blankets and clothes. Textiles symbolized the Korean sense of appreciation, domesticity, good fortune, protection, and wealth. The history of Korean textiles is a portrait of the nation(s).

But this 5000 year heritage took a dark turn in the early 20th century. National ideals were suppressed by mounting pressures in an age of ugly social unrest. Thirty-five years of Japanese colonization had left the nation physically, emotionally, and psychologically damaged. The Korean War of the 1950s was devastating. The reconstruction required a shift from an agricultural economy to a new industrial paradigm. It was a rebirth that challenged the Korean identity and left many unique traditions behind.

Contemporary Korean textile art and its education began at the same time, with only very meagre post-war resources. Shin-Ja Lee, the mother of fiber art in Korea, recalls the period when she had to teach herself how to dye fabrics and invent her own techniques. Sadly, owing to incorrect chemical processes, many of her earlier dyed fabrics and artworks have not been preserved.

Korea has developed so rapidly, particularly in the areas of economy and education. The textile art movement played an increasing role throughout the 1970s and 80s, with the opening of many fiber art programs in colleges, the establishment of fiber art associations and the success of various national competitions. Hugely influential on contemporary Korean textile art have been international exchanges with Europe, Central America, and Japan. Artists like

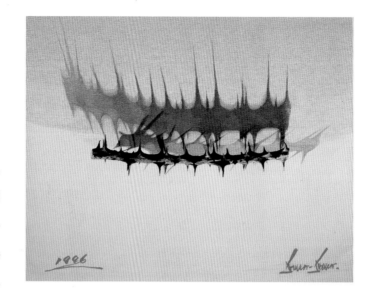

Kea-Nam Cha, Kyung-Yeun Chung, Ja-Hong Ku, Sung-Soon Lee, and Burn-Soo Song all studied overseas. Counterbalancing this, there has also been strong wave of interest in traditional Korean textiles, as well as research on Korean aesthetics, philosophy, and values, exemplified in this book by artists such as Soo-Chul Park, Young-Soon Kim, Kyung-Ae Wang, and later Sung-Soon Lee. This movement has become extremely interesting. Artists pay attention to traditional materials and processes, and have been exploring new ways of translating tradition to their own artwork.

Since the early 1990s, Korea has become a world leader in science and technology. Spurred on by influences from the west, its lifestyle, capitalism, pop-culture, and even its philosophy, the pace of Korean cultural development, self-awareness and self-confidence has quickened. This is reflected in the work of artists such as Ja-Hong Ku, researching on identity and cosmos, and So-Lim Cha, who manifests a chaotic inner voice through contemporary materials and process. The Korean government has been increasingly supportive of the arts, crafts, architecture, and design; with time more and more it is recognizing the valuable and remarkable contributions that cultural activity makes to society.

Contemporary Korean textile art has been introduced to the world through the many artists who have been actively exhibiting internationally since the late 80s. Artists have participated in international touring exhibitions across the USA, Canada, Australia, Russia, and Europe, with the most active exchanges taking place as one would expect in Asia, particularly Japan and more recently China. Artists and educators attend international symposia, giving lectures and workshops. Barely known a decade ago, there has recently been a significant growth in the number of audiences who can now recognize Korean textiles and appreciate its aesthetic.

Chunghie Lee is the best-known ambassador for *Bojagi* and *Jogakbo* throughout the world, through lectures, exhibitions, and workshops. A large western art audience has also recognized Kim Sooja's distinctive video, performance, and installation work. In what is probably her best known video piece, *Cities on the Move – 2727 kilometres Bottari Truck* (1997), she loaded the back of a blue truck with piles of cloth and drove through cities and rural areas in Korea. Do-ho Suh has also come to international prominence lately, exhibiting many large installation pieces throughout the world, and recreating homes and parachutes with textile material and a fibrous process.

Koreans who have so many direct or indirect wounds from the past all have a special attachment to cloth. *Bojagi,* the beautiful and sophisticated Korean cloth, were wrapped bundles of belongings, moved from place to place during the war, clothing stained by dirt, mud, and blood. The bundles served as pillow, blanket, bed, and house, and their own clothes were used to patch their wounds. The textile would age with the passing of time, whether it was red or blue, black or white, and the cloth wrapped and healed those people who needed comfort and remedy. The cloth healed not only bones and sinew but also mind and spirit. Contemporary Korean textile art absorbs the history of the past, attracting and bringing together society, and communicates the psychological conditions of darkness as well as light. History is revealed by textiles.

A distinctive factor in Korean contemporary art is that there has been an almost obsessive interest in the phenomenon of the wound or scar. [1]

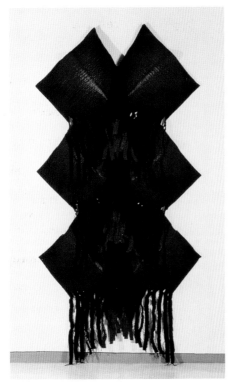

The majority of the artists in this book grew up in what was a time of enormous transition in Korea's history. In the context of the sociological, political, and economic chaos, there was tremendous pressure on the nation simply to survive. Art offered a space for solace: the place for exploring and expressing exhaustion, anxiety, anger, and healing. Textiles was readily approachable for many artists, who could use their domestic environment as their studio with simple tools day and night. Flexibility of time, energy, space, and process has attracted many artists to the contemporary fiber scene in Korea.

For many women, time spent handling cloth was the only time they had to themselves. It would have been all too easy to lose one's identity with so many roles to accomplish: patching children's sleeves, darning holes, sewing on buttons, knitting sweaters, embroidering pillows... Not merely hobbies or simple crafts, these were the very portrait of the woman. In the space provided by textiles, women breathed, dreamed, and were healed.

Shin-Ja Lee's art reflects this. In 1950 she had to face chaos every day in every corner of her home, with a big family and little space. Her art-making was the space to find herself, and she has found the right path. In her painterly embroidery and batik dye works she creates her portrait, using colorful threads to evoke a dreamy scene of women with children, birds, and flowers. Her earlier textile work was closely related to painting with pigment and thread. She has been a supremely productive and motivated artist over five decades in the field.

this page:

Shin-Ja Lee

Harmony

opposite page:

Burn-Soo Song

Self of Wrath

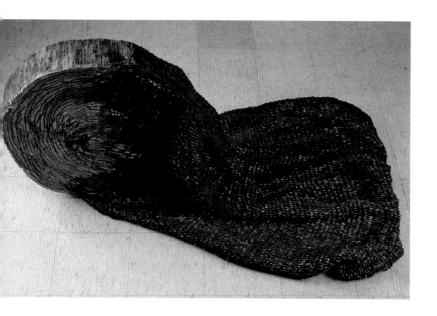

Kyung-Ae Wang's fabric collaged pieces are symbolic manifestations where the stitches appear to heal the fragmented cloth. Her scraps of fabric are ripped, patched, touched. Her magical stitches on the cloth mark the process of healing. This healing may be a political, sociological, or historical one.

So-Lim Cha is the youngest artist among the group, growing up in the 1970s and 80s at the same time as the nation was beginning to develop. But politically Korea continued to have many problems and conflicting situations. Democracy was still in development, the nation in transition. These conflicts are reflected in Cha's work. She uses unconventional materials such as chunks of wood and mirrors, which she reconfigures and transforms until they take on an entirely fresh character. She has woven thousands of zippers, hammering them down into the surface of the wood; the pattern which the zippers create upon the surface of the wood resembles tattoos or scars.

Sophisticated elements of construction in the glove, a symbol of ready-made objects in Korea between the 1950s and the 70s, with their connotations of manual labor, mark the work of glove lady Kyung-Yeun Chung. The interconnectedness of her installations implies an additional, complex layer of our body or skin.

Kea-Nam Cha's layers of dark sisal surfaces are the trace of a wound, a wound that does not want to surface. Those secretive sisal scars are connected to each other. The monumental scale and the division of two geometric scales are the perfect way of hiding the wound as if it never existed. The conflict between the vibrant mark-making on the surface and the solid structure of the underlying form seems to impose a silence on us, the silence of the unspoken question.

The structure of a fabric or its weave – that is, the manner of fastening its constituent elements to each other – is as much a determining factor in its function as is the choice of raw material. In fact, the interrelation of the two, the subtle play between them in supporting, impeding, or modifying each other's characteristics, is the essence of weaving. [2]

Tapestry, the most complex structure of weaving, the methodical building-structure of longitude and latitude, has become the most profound process in the recent history of Korean textile art. Even though the contemporary textile art world may have paid less attention to the tapestry technique since the demise of the

International Lausanne Biennales in the early 1990s, many Korean artists continue to explore this method.

In the Korean language, the first person plural (we, or in Korean *woori*) replaces the first person singular (I, in Korean *na*) in general conversation – unless you are an authority figure. For example, we would say '*our* father' instead of '*my* father', '*our* house' instead of '*my* house', and so forth. I am less important than we are. In Korean culture, this sense of togetherness that is suggested linguistically is fundamental to our national psyche: it could even be described as our national costume.

The structure of weaving and tapestry has been a close equivalent process to demonstrate a social construction based on the importance of shared identity. Tapestry is a continuous process of making *woori*, the harmonious, considered and reflective conjunction of warp and weft. The artist becomes part of the process: their hands and threads have to go through each line of warp yarns and to follow the rhythm; the body stands quietly, just a few inches away, while it is processing. The artist becomes a tapestry.

In the hands of artists such as Burn-Soo Song, Soo-Chul Park, Ja-Hong Ku and Shin-Ja Lee, tapestry has become such a symbol. Many male artists have been deeply involved within the tapestry process, despite there being a ban on male involvement with thread up until the 1970s. In the wake of the war, with its deprivations and starvations, the upbringing of children in general may be

opposite:

So-Lim Cha

Life – Process – Circulation

below:

Kea-Nam Cha

Untitled 5341-3

said to have suffered from the lack of available affection within the family, and in particular from their mother, since everyone was too busy to take care of each other. In this context, thread served as a way of regaining some lost contact, comfort, affection, and love. Culturally Koreans have not been so expressive in their physical touch in public as westerners. The thread has served as a nostalgic metaphor for a mother's arms, her breast, her touch, bringing the fundamental human necessities.

Burn-Soo Song has combined his tapestry imagery with woodcut printing for four decades. His early work is best known for its spontaneous color composition, while his more recent work explores a variety of materials, themes, and approaches. Most recently his *Thorn* series of tapestries represents a psychological investigation into suffering, the evanescence of beauty, and the human condition: the image of the thorn has become an object as well as a subject of stimulation.

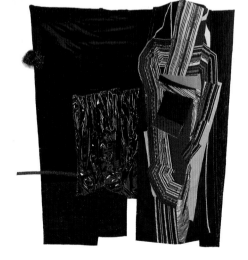

"I grew up with tapestry," writes Soo-Chul Park. He has had a long marriage with the tapestry process in his work. In his early work, Park was very much involved with Korean aesthetics and design: roofs, windows, walls, architecture all afforded him objects worthy for inspiration. His sophisticated sensibility of color and three-dimensional construction brought attention to the essential perfection of structure, like Mondrian.

Ja-Hong Ku's tapestry work shows nostalgic imagery of brushstrokes, flowers, and clouds. But these are deconstructed rather than captured in the center of the space: colors are faded, the composition slips out of focus.

Weaving, tapestry, embroidery, coiling, knitting, netting, and crocheting... These pure repetitive acts have been associated with women's paths down the centuries. Some of these techniques may have developed from social gatherings, or from fundamental needs within people's lives. I believe that the pure and calm movements involved in textile processes have comforted women.

The philosophy of Zen may be practiced through the act of making. With each thread and each knot, these intricate practices may be transformed into a healing remedy: while the body may suffer from the strains of labor, the mind can attain calm and emptiness. This philosophy is fundamental to an understanding of Korean art. Arthur Danto wrote, "I think the basic insights of the Buddha were not somehow peculiar to the East. His thoughts about suffering and release apply to all human beings, and have to do with inescapable problems of being human." [3]

Korea's most famous textile, *Bojagi,* offers space for meditation. *Bojagi* is made from simple patchworks, collage, dye, and embroidery: it can serve a wide variety of different functions.

Young-Soon Kim's gentle and elegant stitches on each small piece of cloth have a sincere emotional touch, while more recently Sung-Soon Lee rides the wave of *Bojagi* with passion and enthusiasm. Through obsessive thread marks, Kyung-Ae Wang finds her metaphor; Kea-Nam Cha fantasizes her nostalgia. So-Lim Cha's intellectual stitches on canvas and cloth broadcast inner strength in the face of chaos.

Ten artists have all chosen textile processes for expressing through their art the anxiety, struggles, and confusion of human life and suffering. The repetitive process itself heals past mistakes and wounds. Meditation and the arts both demonstrate an awakened mind which, together with an essential humanity, they offer to individuals, to society, and even to our cognitive sciences. The humanities have seemed for too long to genuflect before the sciences: but the act of art is such a courageous instrument. Braque once said, "Art is a wound become light". This sensual and humane process of art-making can heal not only its maker but also its viewers. Let us take good care of the field of textiles.

Mi-Kyoung Lee

opposite:

Kyung-Ae Wang

Discrepancy

this page:

Young-Soon Kim

The Endless Reaching Loving Hands 08

Footnotes

1. *Indulgence of Scar: Korean Contemporary Art, Identity and Theory*, by Sun-Hak Kang, Jae Won Publication, 2000.

2. *On Weaving*, by Anni Albers, p. 38, Wesleyan University Press, 1965.

3. By Arthur Danto contributing to *Buddha Mind in Contemporary Art*, Ed. Jacquelyn Baas & Mary Jane Jacobs, University of California Press, 2004.

Kea-Nam Cha

I address material, I listen to its voice, gaze at it, touch it, talk to it, and in turn it gazes at me, touches me. In the middle of this intuitive engagement, the optimum form emerges, as if it were new-born.

Untitled 5337-13

1990

sisal hemp, dyestuff, resin

165 x 310 x 47cm

I started

with a delicate line;

then created a plane, and finally

made a sculptural object. This geometrical

treatment characterizes my work – I treat something

minuscule in just the same way as I treat something huge...

Emptiness is an important concept in oriental philosophies

such as Zen, and in my work also. Knowledge

of emptiness results from a strong wish

to transcend the petty desires and

complications of our

day-to-day life.

above:

Untitled 5339-3 (detail)

1992

sisal hemp, dyestuff, resin

200 x 100 x 700cm

right:

Untitled 5339-1

1992

sisal hemp, dyestuff, resin

260 x 200 x 560cm

Untitled 5348-1

2001

sisal hemp

100 x 75 x 200cm

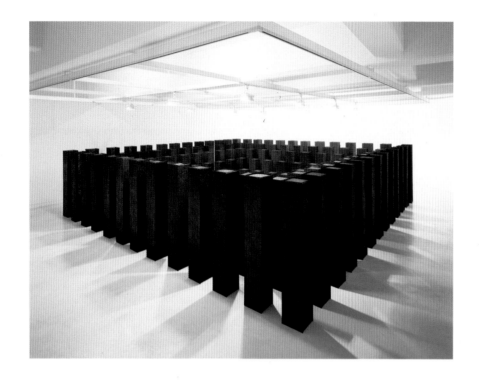

The material reveals itself according to its true nature. It avoids two extremes: neither remaining concealed, nor shouting egotistically. My will and emotions are captured within the material.

The form and colour of the work is represented very simply, excluding any superfluous elements; although I would not describe it as minimalist. I abandoned trying to derive my concept from the exterior; and I chose black, rather than the natural deep colour of hemp.

I imposed this difficult colour on my material, waiting for the time when the material will revive.

top left:

Untitled 5342-1

1995

sisal hemp, dyestuff, resin

625 x 625 x 150cm

bottom left:

Untitled 5341-5

1994

sisal hemp, dyestuff, resin

110 x 110 x 200cm

right:

Untitled 5343-5

1996

sisal hemp, dyestuff, resin

60 x 336 x 193cm

We are invited to enter the private space formed by the relationship between the structure and its surrounding environment, born of material, colour, form, method.

Born   1953, Daegu

Education and Awards

1984   Kyoto City University of Arts, Kyoto, Japan

1992   Excellence Award, International Textile Fair, Kyoto Cultural Museum

1993   Silver Medal, Osaka Triennial, Osaka Cultural Foundation, Osaka

1995   The 7th Ringa Art Prize (artists selection), Tokyo

Selected Solo Exhibitions

2004   Maga Museum, Yongin

2001   Shila Gallery, Daegu

1997   Ghain Gallery, Seoul

1996   Today's Artist Series, Osaka Contemporary Museum, Osaka, Japan

1995   Ci-gong Gallery, Daegu

1994   Gallery Maronie, Kyoto

1993   Ingong Gallery, Seoul

1992   Gallery Maronie, Kyoto

1991   Amano Gallery, Osaka

1990   Kyoni Gallery, Tokyo

1989   Gallery Nakamura, Kyoto

Work in Collection

Busan Metropolitan Art Museum

The National Museum of Art, Osaka

The Museum of Modern Art, Shiga, Ohtsu

Osaka Prefecture, Osaka

National Museum of Contemporary Art, Seoul

The Museum of Kyoto

Phillipse University of Japan, Osaka

Sivaria Museum, Hungary

left:

Untitled 5342-6

1995

sisal hemp, dyestuff, resin

400 x 800 x 400cm

Kyung-Yeun Chung

In America I am known as 'the glove lady'.

left:

Untitled 85-VI

1985

dyed mixed-media on cotton gloves

265 x 214cm

above:

Untitled 04-D

2004

mixed-media on Korean paper

220 x 200cm

left:

Untitled 95-A

1995

dyed mixed-media on

cotton gloves

440 x 120 x 120cm

right:

Untitled 87-1 installation

1987

dyed mixed-media on

cotton gloves

210 x 600cm

below:

Mankind 04-19

2004

mixed-media on Korean paper

151 x 74.5cm

Even though I have experimented with a wide variety of materials over the years, it is my work with gloves that seems to have had the strongest impact on the viewers, and so the name has stuck. A pair of gloves does play a crucial role in my artistic expression, comparable to the role of rice paper in oriental painting, stone in sculpture or canvas in painting.

It all started when my mother sent me a pair of gloves, as a well-intentioned gesture to assist and encourage her hardworking daughter. I in turn dyed a pair of gloves and sent them back to her, to express my gratitude.

The hands of a mother praying for her children; a labourer's sweaty gloves, moulded into the form of the worker's hands… the original functional aspect of a glove is humanised through its use, and takes the shape of an often desperate human life.

The ends of the fingers are produced only in black and white, to express a point. The point, line or plane I desire is human life.

left:

Untitled 85

1985

dyed mixed-media on

cotton gloves

250 x 280cm

right:

Untitled 90-D (detail)

1990

dyed mixed-media on

cotton gloves

200 x 290cm

below:

Untitled 85-V

1985

dyed mixed-media on

cotton gloves

290 x 220cm

Furthermore, it's the creation concept that all things in the universe start as a single point, which gathers to become a line, plane or shape, and in the end return to a point.

Hands for me also make a reference to religion, in particular to Buddhism, which occupies an important place in my life, as a practising Buddhist by upbringing and choice. Concepts such as emptiness, karma, Skandhas and Samadhi have influenced my work and are expressed in my pieces.

From an aesthetic perspective, clay is another important material for me. A symbol of man's earthly origins and ultimate destination, it has traditional significance both as an eastern colour, and as the basis for the manufacture of Korean ceramic tiles. Nature has been a great teacher for me and for my work.

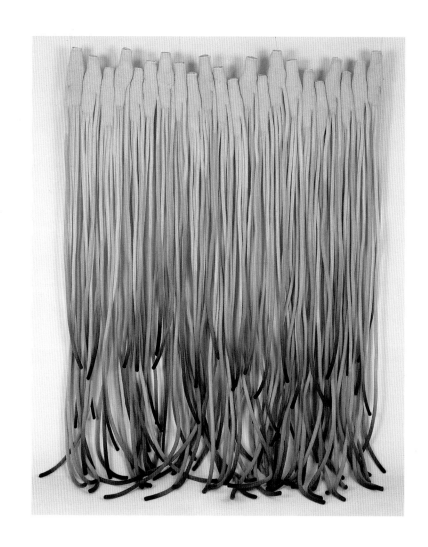

The hands of a mother praying for her children; a labourer's sweaty gloves, moulded into the form of the worker's hands... the original functional aspect of a glove is humanized through its use, and takes the shape of an often desperate human life.

right:

Untitled 80-7 (detail)
1980
dyed mixed-media on
cotton gloves
178 x 345cm

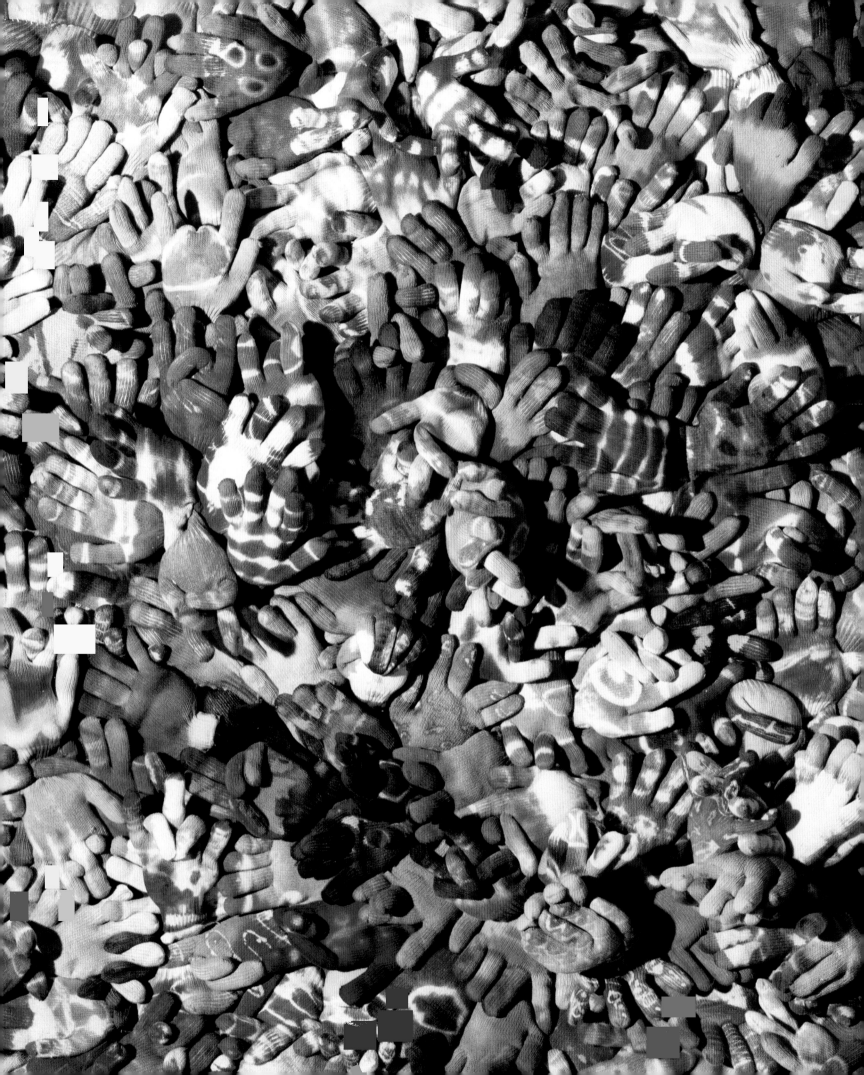

All things in the universe start as a single point, which gathers to become a line, plane or shape, and in the end return to a point.

Born   1955, Busan

Education and Awards

1979	MAE Rhode Island School of Design, Providence
1978	BFA Massachusetts College of Art
1986	Bronze Award, Baghdad International Festival of Art, Spain
1989	Recipient of the First Annual Shaek-Ju Art Award, Seoul
1990	Osaka Triennial '90 Special Award
1996	Honorary Doctoral degree, Moscow S, G Strognov State University of Industry Arts, Russia
2003	MANIF9! 03 Special Award

Selected Exhibitions

2005	Korean Paper Festival, Paris, France
	International Shibori Symposium, Tokyo
	2nd Seoul Contemporary Art Exhibition, Seoul Metropolitan Museum of Artl
2004	Seoul Contemporary Art Exhibition, House of Association of Architecture, Rome
	ICOM Korean Sculpture, The Past & The Future, Hantaek Botanical Garden, Yongin City
	Art Creation, National Museum of History, Taipei (solo)
	38th International Fair for Modern & Contemporary Art, Cologne, Germany
	MANIF 10! 2004, Seoul Art Centre, Seoul (solo)
2003	Pre Documenta, Daegu International Textile Art, Cultural & Art Center, Daegu
1995	Gallery Hankuk, Seoul (solo)

Work in Collection

National Museum of Modern Art, Seoul

Sonjae Museum of Contemporary Art, Kyung-ju

The Museum of Modern Art, Toyama, Japan

Publication

1997	Author: "Contemporary Fiber Art Korea", Chang Mee Publishing Co.
	Translator: "Silk Painting" by Susan Louise Moyer, Kukjae Publishing House

Professional

Currently Professor at Hong-Ik University, Seoul

left:

Untitled 84-7

1984

dyed mixed-media on

cotton gloves

232 x 380cm

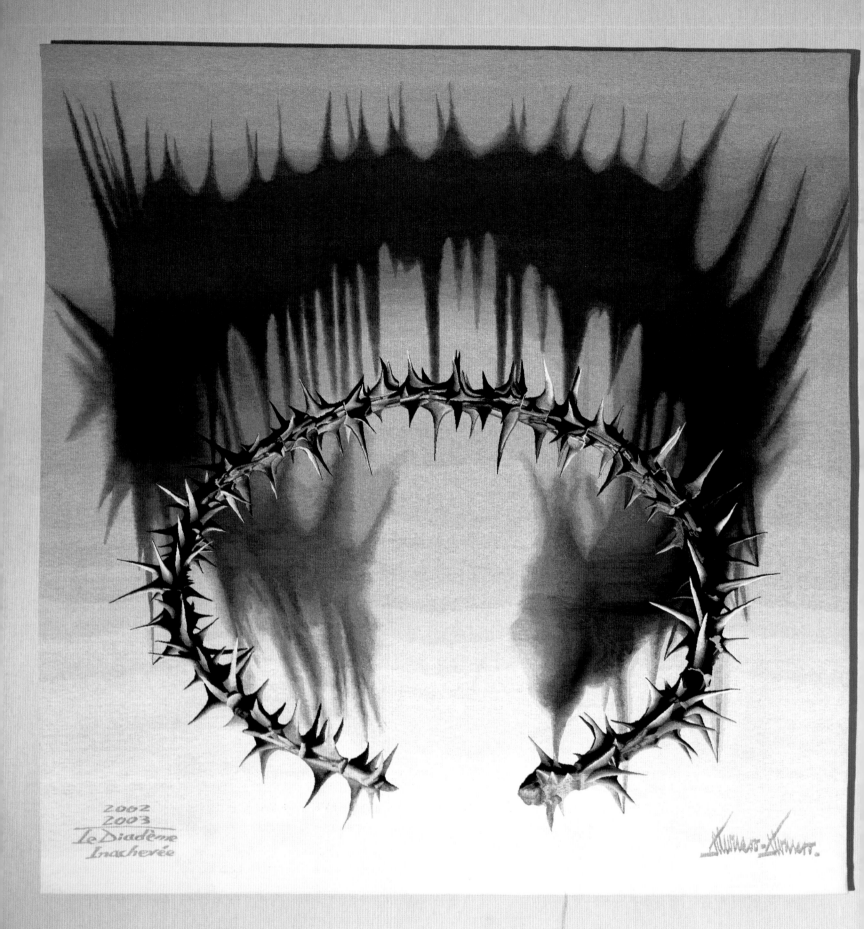

2002
2003
Le Diadème
Inachevée

Burn-Soo Song

Thorns may appear forbidding and harsh. But I feel they
are a truer representation of extreme beauty than the rose.
Although splendid, a rose is more of a temporary illusion.

Le Diadème Inachevée

Neung-Pyong Cathedral Church

2003

wool, plain weaving

400 x 400cm

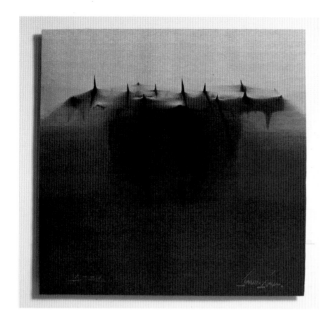

left:

Hopelessness and Possibility
1998
wool, plain weaving
206 x 196cm

I am an artist in pursuit of stimulus through change and development. Nature and the environment are the focus for my expression, which has an ever-present underlay of sensitivity.

My work has taken a wide variety of themes, ranging from the series *The Pre-Designated Bombing Point* from the late 1960s to the 1990 series *The Principle of Relativity.*

Based on my belief that fine arts is a stimulus and the artist must seek change at all times, I have consistently attempted to

interpret the background of my life and times with sensitivity, sublimating it through my work.

It can seem to be unending pain and agony for an artist to express the outcome of mental contemplation visually. There is darkness and sorrow hidden in every corner of my work, with its roots in my personal or social history. I chose to express my son's death, and the socio-political situation of the 1970s and 80s, with vivid colour stimuli rather than through darkness and sorrow, using themes which were sometimes explicit, and at other times metaphorical.

right:

Hopelessness and Possibility
1998
wool, plain weaving
206 x 196cm

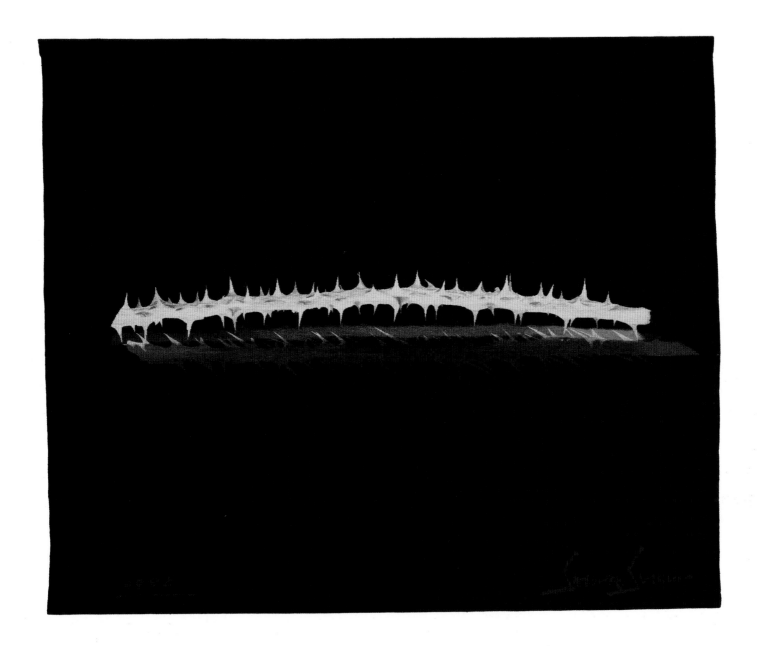

I made the thorns small while enhancing the scale of the shadow,

thus emphasizing the fabricated over the real thorns.

previous page:	above:	right:
An Experienced Truth	**Thawing of Ice**	**Orchestra of Life**
1996	1991	1984
wool, plain weaving	acrylic fibre, plain weaving	acrylic fibre, plain weaving
220 x 270cm	290 x 198cm	280 x 380cm

I always keep my eyes open for something new. My outlook is rather like watching a young child at play and constantly in motion. I reject the limited idea of change where a constant theme is maintained, as there the only change is brought about through the passage of time.

My work aspires to an emphasis on stimulus and freshness of impact. An artist's creative centre is the very thing they wish to express. It is the ultimate assertion of the artist.

When I studied in Paris, I was astonished and awestruck in front of the historical European tapestries. Tapestry is more honest than any other work.

Painting seems relatively predictable in comparison, even though of course there are many different painters. But the medium of woven tapestry brings certain unique constraints through its necessity of a perfect structure, consistent method, physical stamina. And these very constraints can paradoxically allow a breathtaking personal freedom to emerge triumphant. The continuity of work, the methodical application of each weft, charts the course of my life and of my knowledge of art.

My emotional creative world is littered with undetonated grenades. I do not know whether I will take these with me to the grave, or whether they will explode at some point in time into colour and form.

left:

Bloody Mary

1989

hemp and epoxy

three pieces, each 190 x 94cm

above:

The Principle of Relativity

1994

acrylic fibre, plain weaving

302 x 386cm

My emotional creative world is littered with undetonated grenades.

I do not know whether I will take these with me to the grave, or whether

they will explode at some point in time into colour and form.

Born　　　　　1943, Chung Nam, Gong-Ju

Education and Awards

1974　　　MFA Hong-ik University, Seoul

1977　　　National Supérieur des Beaux Arts & Collège d'Enseignement,
　　　　　　Art Graphique, Paris

1986　　　Gold Prize, The 4th Exhibition CS Design, Tokyo

2001　　　First Prize, The 1000th Anniversary of the Foundation of the
　　　　　　Hungarian State, The Hungarian Cultural Heritage, Budapest

2002　　　Honorary Grand Prize, International Tapestry Biennale, Beijing

Selected Exhibitions

2004　　　3rd International Tapestry Biennale, Shanghai Library, Shanghai

2003　　　Crossings 2003: Korea-Hawaii, Honolulu Academy of Arts, Hawaii
　　　　　　Tanaka Hideo & Song Burn Soo, Contemporary Art Niki, Tokyo
　　　　　　Invitational Exhibition, the opening of Shaekdam Museum,
　　　　　　Songdam University, Yongin City (solo)

2002　　　2nd International Tapestry Biennale, Beijing

1999　　　Kyoto Museum of Cultural Centre, Kyoto (solo)
　　　　　　Il Min Museum of Art, Seoul (solo)

1994　　　Total Museum of Contemporary of Art, Seoul (solo)

Work in Collection

National Museum of Contemporary Art, Seoul

National Museum of Fine Arts, Budapest, Hungary

Korea Headquarters of Geneva, Swiss

Samsung Medical Centre, Seoul

Daejeon City Museum of Art, Daejeon

Publications

1996　　　Author: "Contemporary Fiber Art", Worlgan Design, Seoul

1991　　　Author: "Actuality of Dyeing", Mijinsa, Seoul

1985　　　Author: "Fiber Art", Worlgan Design, Seoul

Professional

Currently　　　Professor at Hong-ik University, Seoul

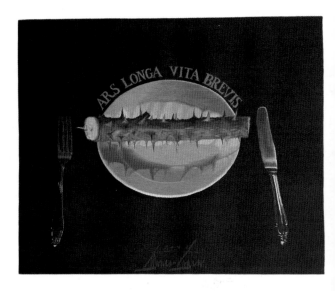

Artist's Last Supper

2002

wool, plain weaving

197 x 243cm

Young-Soon Kim

My artwork presents the image of traditional Korean wrapping cloth while reflecting modern aesthetics.

left:

The Endlessly Reaching Loving Hands 01

1988

natural dyes, ramie, hemp, hand-stitching

90 x 90cm

above:

The Endlessly Reaching Loving Hands 21

2002

natural dyes, ramie, embroidery yarn, patchwork, hand- and machine-embroidery

160 x 160cm

For more than 30 years I have been exploring the new possibilites of 'The Beauty of *Bojagi*' (wrapping cloth) by re-interpreting the image of *Jogakbo* (a traditional Korean women's handicraft of patchwork wrapping cloth). Traditionally, wrapping cloth was used to wrap or cover objects, and traditional patchwork wrapping cloth was made in such a way as to patch diverse pieces of cloth for practical use. I am reinterpreting the image of traditional Korean patchwork wrapping cloth, and presenting it as an aesthetic object of my own.

Since my youth, I have been blessed with talents and interested in making objects. Being attracted to making such objects, whilst interested in soft fibre as an artistic material in its own right, it was only natural that I should come to major in fibre art, also known as 'The Art of Women'.

The nostalgia that arises from the memory of my mother making my *Hanbok* (Korean costume) with her own hands is the motive of my work. Some of my inspiration comes from my childhood memories of my mother engaged with *Jogakbo*. Most of my works are handmade, something I have in common with an earlier generation of women who sewed stitch-by-stitch to make a patchwork wrapping cloth. Since the main theme of my work is '*Endless Hand Touch*', I attempt to reflect women's experiences in the process of reviving my *Jogakbo*. In this series, the sides of the patchwork are organized with geometric figures as triangles, squares, rectangles and lozenges. These figures are presented not in a hard-edged manner, but in a gentle and natural way; the position of the colours is based on the harmony of the Five Colours, monochromatic colours and pastels which project Korea's intrinsic sensibility.

left:

The Endlessly Reaching Loving Hands 16

2002

natural dyes, ramie, hemp, silk, embroidery yarn, patchwork, hand- and machine-embroidery

206 x 206cm

right:

The Endlessly Reaching Loving Hands 02

1988

natural dyes, ramie, embroidery yarn, hemp, patchwork, hand-stitching

88 x 88cm

above:

The Endlessly Reaching Loving Hands 07

1991

natural dyes, ramie, embroidery yarn, hand-made

paper, patchwork, hand-embroidery

158 x 154cm

right:

The Endlessly Reaching Loving Hands 05

1991

natural dyes, ramie, hemp, hand-made paper,

embroidery yarn, patchwork, hand-embroidery

125 x 130cm

The sides of the patchwork are organized with geometric figures as triangles, squares, rectangles and lozenges. These figures are presented not in a hard-edged manner, but in a gentle and natural way; the position of the colours is based on the harmony of the Five Colours, monochromatic colours and pastels which project Korea's intrinsic sensibility.

above:

The Endlessly Reaching Loving Hands 23

2004

natural dyes, ramie, embroidery yarn,

knotting, beads, watch, patchwork,

hand- and machine-embroidery

variable dimensions, each approx. 14 x 14 x 8cm

left:

The Endlessly Reaching Loving Hands 22

2004

natural dye matiere, ramie, embroidery yarn,

patchwork, hand-stitching, machine-embroidery

each 17 x 17 x 10cm

My fibre works are based on natural dyeing, mainly using environmentally-friendly materials like ramie or hemp cloth. The poem *Green Grape* by Korean poet Lee Yook-Sa says "My dear child, let us be prepared on our table with a silver plate, and on the silver plate, a white white ramie handkerchief". I make patchwork wrapping cloth by cutting and patching the pieces of ramie and hemp cloth that I dyed with natural dye. The patchwork wrapping cloth, consisting of natural dyed cloth pieces, forms a natural colourful harmony which appears to be the Yin-Yang symbol plus the Five Elements. I use techniques such as patchwork, hand-stitching, hand-embroidery, machine-embroidery, roller print moulding, and salasa. I also attempt to apply diverse techniques using Korean paper, knots, beads and thread partially on pieces of patchwork wrapping cloth after cutting and patching hemp, Korean paper and silk, hand-dyed and woven myself.

Born   1947, Seoul

Education and Awards

1976   MFA, Hong-ik University, Seoul

1983   Invited Artist, The 6th Korean Arts & Culture Exhibition,

              Paris Salon De Me, Selected Association of Korea

1985   Certified Degree, Ecole des Beaux-Arts, Fontainebleau, France

2001   'Choo-ge' Artist Award, Seoul

Selected Exhibitions

2004   COEX Indian Ocean Hall, Convention & Exhibition, Seoul (solo)

              'Image of Living' Korean-Japanese Artists, Baik-Song Art Gallery, Seoul

2003   Daegu Textile Art Pre-Documenta 2003, Cultural Centre, Daegu

2002   Milestone Art Works, Toyama, Japan (solo)

              Invited Exhibition: 'Beauty of Korea', Turkey

2001   Busan International Textile & Fashion Show, Busan

1999   Cheongju International Crafts Biennial, Art Centre, Cheongju

              NICAF TOKYO, The 6th International Contemporary Art Festival, Tokyo

1998   The Sounds of Korea-Fiber Art Show, Museum of the City of Lodz, Poland

1997   Jung-gu Cultural Centre, Daejeon (solo)

Work in Collection

Smithsonian Museum, Washington D.C.

Toyama Design Centre, Toyama, Japan

Contemporary Art Museum of Hong-ik University, Seoul

Daejeon Municipal Museum of Art, Daejeon

Huh Dong Wha Museum, Seoul

Gallery Sagas Sagas, Kobe, Japan

Professional

Currently Professor at MokWon University, Daejeon

left:

The Endlessly Reaching Loving Hands 12

1991

natural dyes, ramie, embroidery

yarn, knotting, thimble

65 x 65cm

Ja-Hong Ku

Tapestry is a reflection of my life.

left:

A Cloud (detail)

1988

cotton, wool, tapestry

3.7 x 3m

above:

A Sunflower (detail)

1989

cotton, wool, tapestry

3.7 x 3m

left:

Gladness I

1998

cotton, wool, tapestry

1.3 x 1.3m

right:

Gladness II

1999

cotton, wool, tapestry

1 x 1m

When I was young, I was blessed with a combination of passion
and courage: that courage sought a more mature identity, and
the passion searched for the meaning of life.

When I was young, I loved the sea, with its horizon so far distant
and stretching, spreading eternally. It made no difference
whether I was swimming in the sea, or in a boat on top of it,
I always felt that I missed it, so intense was my desire for it.
I tried to give a form to express its sounds and movements:
I alighted on birds, migratory birds spreading their wings,
and my heart melted, a weight was lifted.

I added more depth with simple brush strokes, and a square setting, like a picture frame, into the dynamic tapestry. This gave the visual effect of simplicity to what before seemed an uncertain pattern.

With the image of the globe, I am referring to the co-existence of many different planets, each tracing its own path: within individual freedom there is a universal order and framework.

above:

Space I

2001

silk, styrofoam, pins, coiling

5 x 7m

right:

Existence II

2000

cotton, wool, tapestry

1 x 1m

I yearn to express the sea's waves; the human heart; birds and our human mind; birds and waves. I use fluid shapes, and I distinctly separate red,
yellow, blue and black. I had found an image which inspired and expressed my feeling of fluid movement, of transformation.

I added more depth with simple brush strokes, and a square setting, like a picture frame, into the dynamic tapestry. This gave the visual effect of simplicity to what before seemed an uncertain pattern.

In the day to day business of normal life, I sensed that something had been lost: the heart, wishing to rediscover, was able to concentrate on tthe mysterious power of the universe seeking the origins of life.

right:
Space III
2003
silk, styrofoam, pin, coiling
1 x 1m

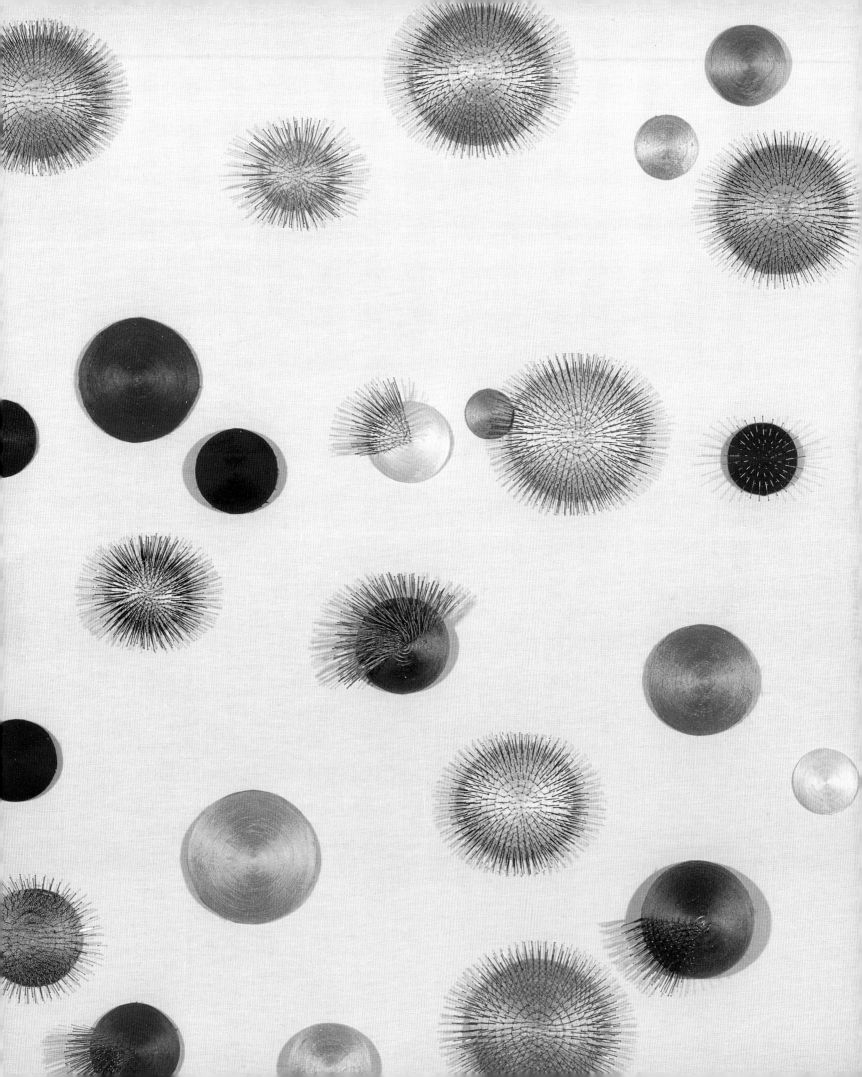

A path stretches before me, a long journey knowing no limits,

in pursuit of the origin of life and of universal creation.

Born 1954, Jinju

Education and Awards

M.A. Dong-A University, Busan

1983 Excellence Prize, Busan Arts Grand Exhibition, Busan

1986 Gold Medal, Korea Craft Grand Exhibition, Busan

1992 Grand Prize, Korea Craft Grand Exhibition, Busan

2000 Art and Science, Nominated work, Beijing, China

2004 Fiber Art International 2004 , Pittsburgh, USA

Selected Exhibitions

2004 International Fiber Arts Biennial Exhibition,

Museum of Art and Design, New York

'From Lausanne to Beijing', International Tapestry Biennial, Beijing

2002 10th Korean Fiber Arts Biennial, Seoul

2001 University of Georgia & Dong-A University Exchange Exhibition,

Athens, USA

2000 Youngdo International Environmental Art Festival, Busan

Korean Textile Design Association Exhibition, Seoul

Busan Art Festival International Tapestry Art Exhibition, Busan

1999 Daegu International Fiber Design Exchange Exhibition,

Cultural Centre, Daegu

1998 '-trans' Fiber Works in Miniature Exhibition, Network Gallery & NC Gallery, Bloomfield Hills & Busan

Work in Collection

1999 Cultural Art Centre, Stage Curtain, Kumi

Professional

Currently Dean of College of Art and Professor, Dong-A University, Busan

Space V (detail)
2003
silk, styrofoam, pins, coiling

Soo-Chul Park

I have been fascinated by the structure of tapestry, both by its systematic ordering and by the texture formed by layers of yarn.

left and above:

Formation 87-2

1987

wool, tapestry

240 x 340cm

left:

Exhibition in Busan

Metropolitan Art Museum

2000

below:

Busan Cultural Centre

Grand Hall Stage Curtain

1988

wool, tapestry

1000 x 2000cm

Tapestry weaving is a very noble process, which allies self-expression and self-discipline. For some 30 years I have been fascinated by the structure of tapestry, both by its systematic ordering and by the texture formed by layers of yarn. Tapestry is now a reflection of my life; I have grown up with tapestry. It has become my strength and my very breath.

My earlier expression in textiles was inspired by my strong interest in traditional Korean culture and by traditional imagery, such as the beautiful Korean slate roofs, and the characteristic windows made from rice-paper. My eye was captivated by their simplicity and repetitive structure. My ideology about creation is harmonized and integrated by Korean imagery. It is given a modern twist through varied modes and tropes by which cubes, planes and rectangles can be integrated.

After a decade of those preoccupations, I moved towards much simpler compositions using strong colours and curved lines within a frame, seen as if from the outside. Then I applied smaller units to create a larger scale of repetition.

Tapestry is now a reflection of my life; I have grown up with
tapestry. It has become my strength and my very breath.

above:
Transformation 99-1
with the Artist
1999
wool, tapestry
240 x 400cm

pages 66-67, 70:
In-Cheon Cultural Centre
Grand Hall Stage Curtain
1993
wool, tapestry
20 x 10m

Recently I have been developing photo-realistic documentation pieces, woven in tapestry, using my collection of photographs. The subjects include those people with whom I have been connecting, some of them colleagues, sharing precious moments together.

My thread has been travelling with me to create many extremely controlled abstract images, and now it is creating memories: memories of truth about my history, your history, and our history. I believe the power of textiles is, at least in part, that it cultivates a sense of nostalgia in us.

I have been very strongly influenced by my mentor Kwhang-Yeoul Yoo. He was one of the most inspiring people in my education. I wish that I could be an educator like him.

Textiles cultivate a sense of nostalgia in us. The colours, textures, smells, softness, intimacy, all stem from the resource which is our childhood experiences, a place to which we can never return in this lifetime.

bottom left:

Kwhang-Yeoul Yoo

2004

wool, tapestry

100 x 100cm

top left:

Gerhardt Knodel. Professor

2005

wool, tapestry

80 x 80cm

above:

My Family in 1982

2003

wool, tapestry

90 x 160cm

Many of my commissioned pieces were challenging in terms of working with so many colleagues and interns.

Born   1947, Busan

Education and Awards

1975	MFA Hong-ik University, Seoul
1981	A Grand Prize, The 30th Korean National Art Exhibition, Seoul
2003	A Special Popular Prize, Hong-ik Fibre & Plastic Art Association, Seoul
2004	Distinguished Service in Education Prize, Busan

Selected Solo Exhibitions

2004	GuanShanYue Art Museum, Shenzhen, China
2003	Fukuoka Metropolitan Art Museum, Fukuoka, Japan
2001	Georgia Museum of Art, University of Georgia, Athens, USA
1999	N.C. Gallery, Busan
1995	Busan Cultural Centre, Busan
1991	Gallery Space 21, Tokyo
1987	Catholic Centre Art Museum, Busan

Work in Collection

Shenzhen Polytechnic, Shenzhen

Guan ShanYue Art Museum, Shenzhen

Busan Metropolitan Art Museum, Busan

Modern Museum of Hong-ik University, Seoul

Art Museum of Academy of Art & Design, Tsinghua University, Beijing

Taipei City Museum, Taipei, Taiwan

Korea Modern Art Museum, Seoul

Commissions

1995	Manufacture of Stage Curtain, Ku-Mi Cultural & Art Centre– Grand Hall, Ku-Mi
1994	Manufacture of Stage Curtain, Chi-Ak Art Centre – Grand Hall, Won-Ju
1993	Manufacture of Stage Curtain, In-Cheon Cultural Centre – Grand & Middle Halls, In-Cheon
1991	Design and manufacture of Stage Curtain, Busan Cultural Centre – Small Hall, Busan
1988	Design and manufacture of Stage Curtain, Busan Cultural Centre – Grand Hall, Busan

Professional

Currently Professor at Dong-A University, Busan

Sung-Soon Lee

Through stitching and dyeing, I have tried to express the intimate relationship of material and colour in a visual and emotional space of tactility and flexibility.

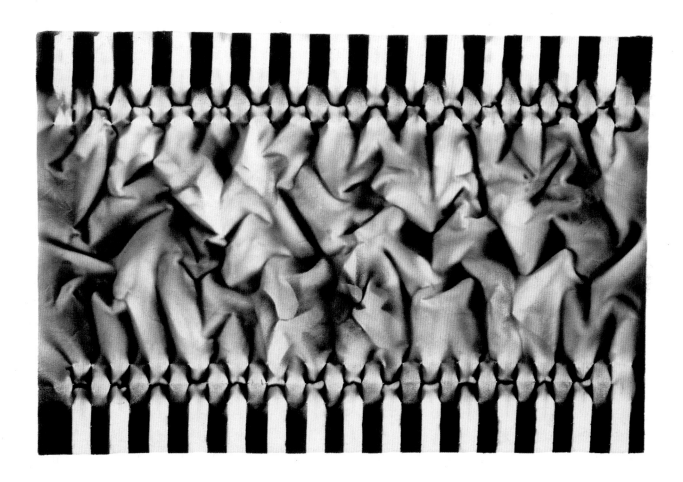

left:

Glory to You
1998
stitching, drawing and
dyeing on velveteen
110 x 110cm

above:

Pioneers
1995
stitching, drawing and
dyeing on velveteen
80 x 110cm

Through a balance of stitching and dyeing, and through an updated shibori technique, I yearn to modernize Korean textile art. The forms expressed reveal the structural beauty of our traditional folk art, such as bamboo basketry or straw bags.

My work expresses a wide variety of social issues and issues in my daily life, including my mother's death; yearning for my two children; an encounter with God; the existence of Kwang-Hwa-Moon; the tensions that can arise from cultural differences of the East and West; gender discrimination; the effects of acid rain and pollution; even the 2002 Seoul World Cup.

The second stage is a textile expression that attempts to transform maternal instincts into a space of soft aesthetics that can best be expressed through stitching. Softness is the source of life that historically formed the cycle of nature, an organic mode of life, and the warm relationship among organisms.

above:

Long Journey & Rest
1995
stitching, drawing and
dyeing on velveteen
300 x 40cm

right:

Silent People
1995
stitching, drawing and
dyeing on velveteen
220 x 110cm

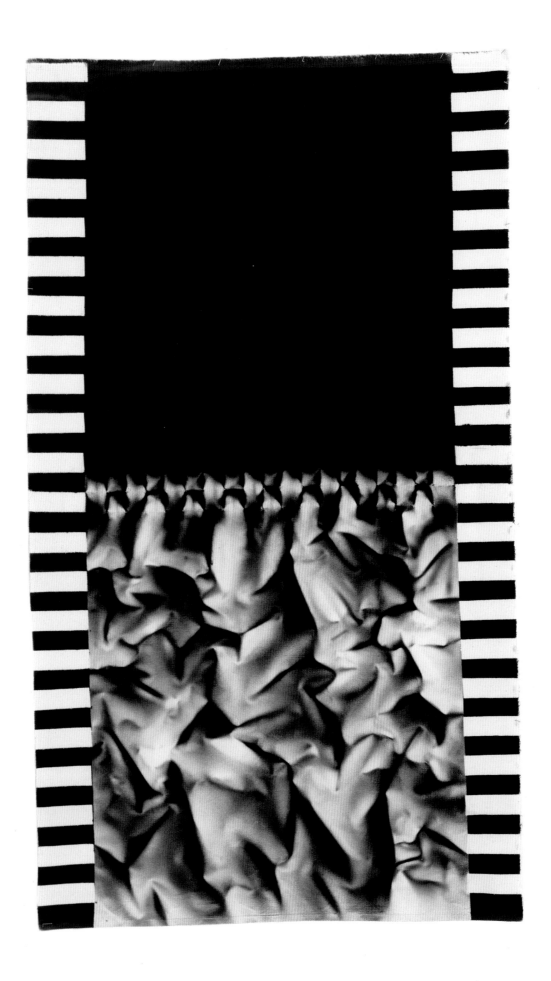

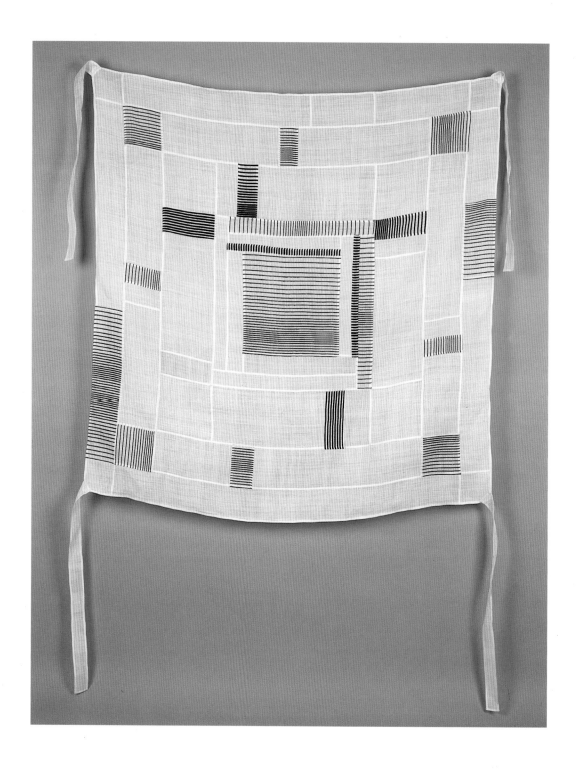

above:

Seon III

2004

drawing, printing and

patchwork on ramie

150 x 150cm

right:

Seon I

2004

drawing, printing and

patchwork on ramie

90 x 60cm

Bojagi is a traditional Korean patchwork technique of wrapping cloth, or more specifically ramie fabric or silk. Ramie seems to have the clarity of the air we breathe: its transparent atmosphere purifies my soul. My work attempts to achieve a state of Zen.

In the past I polluted pure water and clean air while dyeing fabric. Now I deeply regret my actions. It is my wish that my umbrellas will shield us from acid rain; that fish may come back to our rivers; and that we will again be able to breathe the fresh air below the deep Blue Mountains.

above:

Shielding Us from Acid Rain
1999
dyeing and hand printing on fabric
installation (199 umbrellas)

right:

Shielding Us from Acid Rain
1997
dyeing and hand printing on fabric
installation (33 umbrellas)

Seon evokes many things: virtue, the first, a meeting, a choice, a track,

a level and a line. I invite you to my art space. Art in Bojagi – Fabric in Art.

Born   1943, Tokyo

Education and Awards

1967	MFA, Ewha Woman's University, Seoul
1978	BFA, The School of the Art Institute of Chicago, Chicago
1979	International Miner & Chemical Corporation Award, Chicago
1996	Korean Crafts Council Award, Seoul
1997	Vermont Residency Grant, Vermont Studio Center, USA
2000	Fulbright Senior Research Scholar,
	Research at The School of the Art Institute of Chicago
	Mokyang Craft Award – Korean Craft Council

Selected Solo Exhibitions

2005	'Fiber Art Exhibition', Wacoal Ginza Art Space, Tokyo
2004	'Fiber-Bojagi Installation', Berozkina Gallery, Seattle
	'Art in House – Fabric in Art', Hyun Woo Design, Seoul
	'Seon', Gallery Mokkumto, Seoul
2000	'Fiber Art Installation', Walsh Gallery, Chicago
1999	'Shielding Us from Acid Rain', Hanam Environment Expo, Hanam
1998	'The Exhibition of Umbrellas', Hand & Mind, Seoul
1998	'Compositions on Fabric', Hyundai Art Gallery, Seoul
1997	'Compositions on Fabric', The Kookjae News Cultural Centre, Busan
1995	'Compositions on Fabric', Yuna Gallery, Seoul

above:

My Work Begins with Needlework

1997

stitching on velveteen

110 x 110cm

Work in Collection

National Museum of Contemporary Art, Seoul

Seoul Museum of Art, Seoul

Seoul College of the Arts, Seoul

The School of the Art Institute of Chicago, Chicago

Citicorp – Citibank, Seoul

previous page:

Seon - VI

2004

ramie, drawing, printing and patchwork

variable installation

Professional

Currently Professor at Ewha Woman's University, Seoul

Shin-Ja Lee

*I have sought to recreate the beauty of nature intuitively
in my work, using the unique tactile effects of textiles.*

left:

Conversation of Autumn

1977

felt, cotton thread, free technique,

sewing, stitch, dyestuff

140 x 240 x 3cm

above:

Sentiment in Autumn

1987

wool, synthetic thread,

tapestry

151 x 223cm

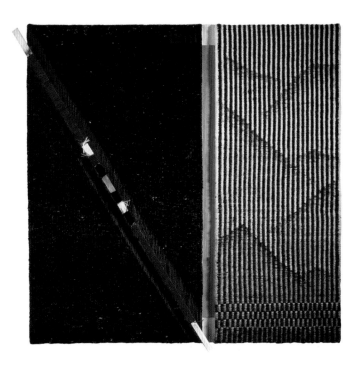

left:

Hope 1

2002

wool, thread, copper,

cotton yarn, coiling, soumak

65 x 65 x 7cm

right:

Echo

1990

wool, synthetic thread,

tapestry

110 x 105cm

As a child, I played with the clothing and thread in my mother's basket and was amazed by the beautiful patterns that my grandmother made with her spinning and weaving machine. This is how I began working with textiles.

In the 1960s I passionately dyed and wove fabric to establish my artistic identity. I tried my best to lead the trend of textiles in Korea. As a professor at a university, I cultivated future artists and was awarded four prizes in the National Arts Exhibition and from the Ministry of Education. I also participated in the National Arts Exhibition as a juror and an operation committee member until 1981.

By serving as a juror and operation committee member of the Korea Industrial Design Exhibition from 1966 to 1991, I took a leading role in the new trend of design in Korea. As a dean of an art school, I taught my students passionately and did my utmost in cultivating a new area in textiles. So many art students I taught at the time are now widely active in this area.

Through my 50 year career, I experienced several transformations in style. The artistic aim that I have been pursuing is based on nature as the origin of creation. Using my intuitive approach, I recreated the beauty of nature in my work by using the unique tactile effect of textiles.

By adopting a variety of painting techniques, I am working on expressing a three-dimensional effect in two-dimensional work.

Since retirement from the university, I have been working on tapestry as the only textile artist at The National Academy of Korean Arts, and as the Director of The Wooduk Cultural Centre, I have been curating exhibitions. My recent works focus on creating certain patterns by the repetition of intense streaks or by simplified division.

By adopting various painting techniques I am working on expressing a three-dimensional effect in two-dimensional work. I am approaching a ripe stage in my life. Just like all creative artists, I wish to leave my mark in the world and hope my effort to realize this desire will be remembered.

page 86:

Beginning of the Universe

1988

wool, synthetic thread,

tapestry

115 x 310cm

page 87:

Plaer I

1985

wool, thread, felt, cloth, tapestry,

slit, fringe, knot

430 x 110 x 5cm

above and left:

The Han River Life Vein of Seoul

1990-1993

wool, synthetic thread, tapestry

65 x 1870cm

My recent works focus on creating certain patterns by the repetition of intense streaks or by simplified division.

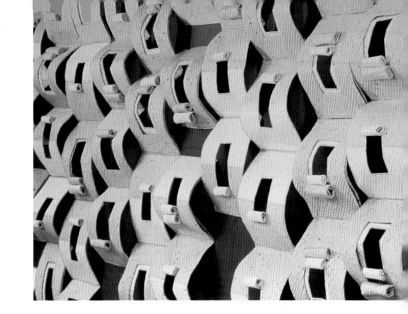

Born   1931, Wooljin, Kyungbuk

Education and Awards

      MFA Hong-ik University, Seoul

1995   Special Culture Award from the Korean Government

1999   Silver Crown Metal for Culture from the Korean Government

2002   National Academy of Korean Arts, the Republic of Korea

Selected Exhibitions

2004   Daegu Textile Art Documenta, Cultural Centre, Daegu

2003   'Breath of Nature', Korean International Exchange Foundation, Saint Petersburg, Russia

      '2003 Crossing: Korea at Hawaii', Academy of Hawaii

2001   'Shin-Ja Lee Tapestry', Seoul Art Centre, Seoul (solo)

2000   International Joint Exhibition for Fiber Arts of Indonesia/Korea, Jakarta Textile Museum

1998   'Comparaisons: Paris – l'Art Actuel', Paris

1995   15 Contemporary Korean Clay, Metal & Fiber Artists, Arizona & Pittsburgh Museum

1989-91   'Land of Morning Calm', Korean Metal & Fiber Artists, USA and Canada

Selected Collections

National Museum of Contemporary Art, Seoul

Seoul Metropolitan Museum of Art, Seoul

Hoam Art Museum, Seoul

Daejeon City Museum of Art, Daejeon

The Kuwait Embassy, Seoul

Professional

Member of the National Academy of Korean Arts

Professor Emeritus of Duksung Women's University

Director of Wooduk Cultural Centre

opposite:

Joining of Squares

2004-5

copper, cotton yarn,

wood, wool coiling

75 x 175 x 7cm

above:

Gracefulness in White

1983

copper, paper, cotton, sponge

machine embroidery, stitch

250 x 500 x 10cm

Kyung-Ae Wang

*Fabric approaches me as if it wants
me to understand its meaning.*

left:
Nativity (detail)
2002
cotton, gauze, free technique
installation

above:
Impromptu Amusement 9005
1990
hemp, cotton, gauze, fabric collage
200 x 150cm

elaborately embroidered fabric boasts of its wealth. Holding a torn piece of fabric in my hands, I can sense and share its pain. Seeing somebody's clothes hanging on the line, I can interpret them to understand the owner's life and personality. I am in awe and admiration for fabric, in all its adaptability and diversity.

Fabric approaches me as if it wants me to understand its meaning. The memory of a thread, detached from a worn sleeve worn by my mother, has become in my mind an emblem: conjuring up my sense of yearning for her, my memories of my childhood, and my intimate attachment to fabric.

Fabric is a special material which has a strong appeal, thanks to its unique sensitivity and expressiveness. But what does it express? When I take the scissors to a piece of fabric, I imagine that I am cutting away conflict; when I put together pieces of fabric, I feel that I am creating harmony and unity; an old fabric reveals the wrinkles of accumulated history; while an

Sometimes I feel that I would love to be wrapped up in a giant piece of fabric!

top left:

Rags 9311

1993

fabrics, needle work,

dyeing, quilting

160 x 180 x 35cm

bottom left:

Impromptu

Amusement 1-90

1990

fabrics, fabric collage

135 x 100cm

above:

Rags 9621

1996

cotton, cotton pad, assorted fabrics,

needle work, dyeing, quilting

375 x 617cm

The problems and conflicts that a person encounters while growing-up and entering society may often be best explored through the medium of art, rather than being tackled head-on. Art offers a safe haven for contemplating the issues symbolically and subliminally.

above:

Nativity

2002

installation: cotton gauze,

free technique,

7 x 3 x 3m

right:

From a Dot 0002

2002

cotton, cotton pad,

hand-quilting

60 x 80cm

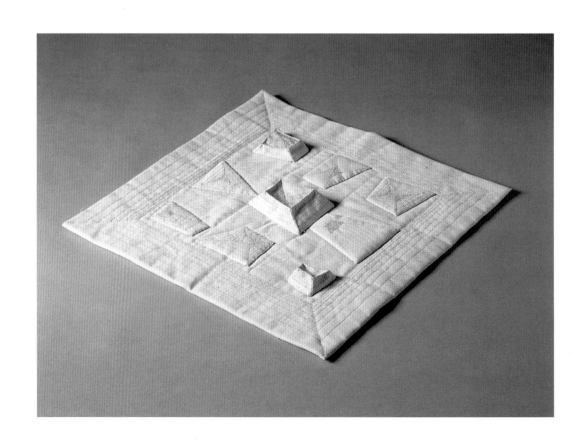

above:

The Earth 0001

2000

cotton, cotton pad,

hand-quilting

97 x 168cm

pages 98-99:

Rags 9626

1996

variety of fabrics, sewing,

dyeing, quilting

340 x 465 x 13cm

Fabric is a material offering consolation through its softness and warm textures. It is
my wish that I will be able to embrace life and meet its difficulties with suppleness,
and learn to live a harmonious life by learning the temperaments of fabric as my own.

Born 1955, Busan

Education

1981	MFA Hong-ik University, Seoul
2002–	PhD Art Theory, Hong-ik University, Seoul *(in progress)*

Selected Exhibitions

2005	12th Solo Exhibition, Gallery Sang, Seoul
	Japan & Korean Exchange Basketry Exhibition, Isakawa, Japan
	2nd Korea Art Quilt, Mok • Kum • To Gallery, Seoul
2004	Installation, Heyri Festival Open Space, Paju
	Difference and Gap, Its Assemblage, Hong-Ik Modern Gallery, Seoul
	Daegu Textile Art Documenta, Daegu Convention Centre, Daegu
	Seoul Art Exhibition, Seoul Museum of Art
2003	Saint Petersburg 300th year Memorial Exhibition, Russia
	The 8th Busan Textile Design Contest, Busan Convention Centre
2002	Busan International Fiber and Fashion Art Festival,
	Busan Convention Centre
	International Tapestry Biennale, Beijing
2000	Art EXPO, New York
1999	Chungju International Crafts Biennial, Chungju
	Women's Art Festival '99: Patjis on Parade, Seoul Art Centre, Seoul
1998	Media & Site, Busan Metropolitan Museum of Art Grand Open Exhibition

Work in Collection

Hoam Art Museum, Seoul

Hong-ik Modern Gallery, Seoul

Busan Museum of Modern Art, Busan

Maga Museum, Yongin City

ALKA Gallery, Vladivostok, Russia

Professional

Currently Professor at Dong-A University, Busan

opposite:

Rags 9603
1996
variety of fabrics, sewing,
dyeing, quilting
305 x 556 x 60cm

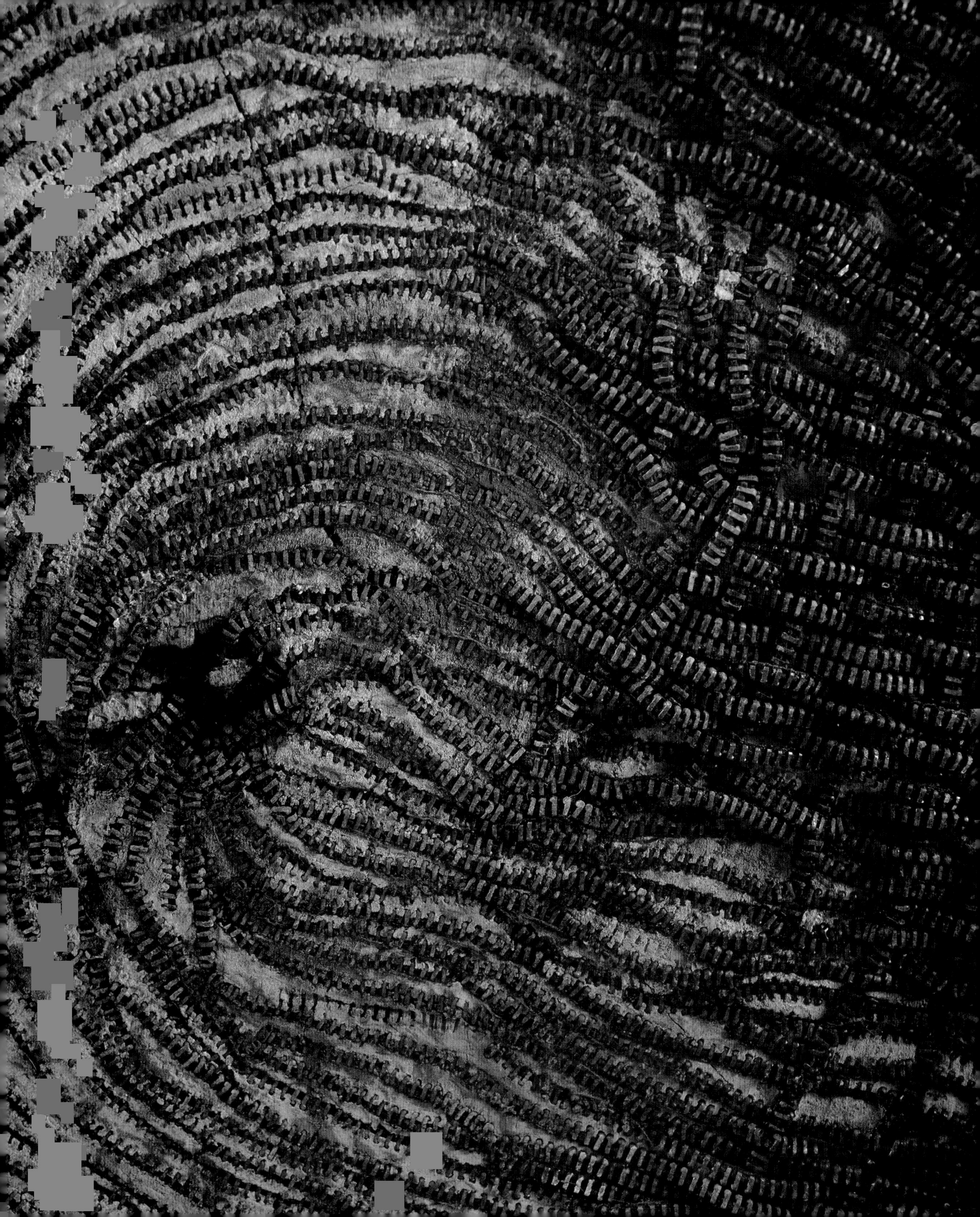

So-Lim Cha

*Through metaphor and symbol I show the process through which
two seemingly opposed elements may be unified: darkness and light;
the natural and the man-made; depth and surface; injury and healing.*

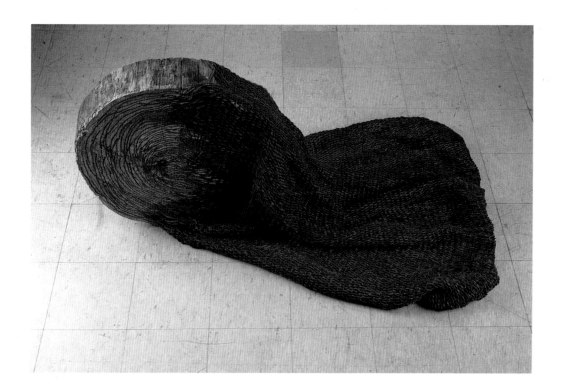

above:

Life – Process – Circulation

1997

wood, nail, zip, rust

70 x 180 x 120cm

My studio is a place where I conceive and realize my work. Where I only have ears for my inner voice. My thinking is expressed as a drawing, often constructed on canvas. It is embodied in space in a variety of materials. It might be that I hew a tree, and hammer metal or iron into it; or I might wind thread onto a canvas; or I might use video to convey

drive a zip or a nail, over and over again, into a tree: over time they are changed. This process reveals the nature of cyclical existence. Humankind enjoys a symbiotic relationship with the outer world: one might often identify oneself with emotions which have arisen in reaction to a stimulus from the outside world. The specific, repetitive

movement, sound. The final choice of materials and techniques results from a lengthy process of trial and error, and is dependent on finding the closest possible correlation of my internal and bodily rhythms to its most appropriate mode of visual realization. For example, I might

rhythms of my body – heartbeat, breath and so forth – form an important basis for my work, since organic outward forms result from instinctive bodily patterns. A striking visual image is formed by a repetitive action, translating an inner voice into a visual creation.

above:
Life – 33
1995
wood, nail, cotton, bandage
33 pieces, each 50 x 15 x 10cm

right:
Healing (detail)
2001
wood, zip, nail, plaster, epoxy
125 x 35 x 4cm

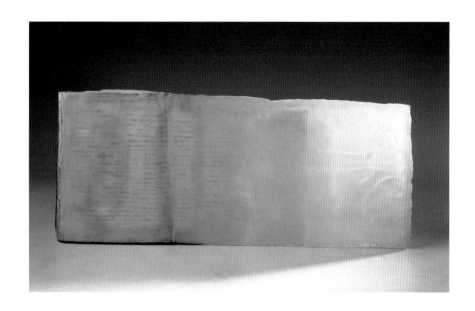

*I wish to uncover the hidden
code which we all seek,
presenting it as an image.*

above:

creation – code

2002

wood, epoxy, plaster

27 x 64 x 4cm

right:

emptiness – code (detail)

2002

plaster, epoxy

four pieces, each 28 x 22 x 3cm

left:

Message (detail)

2004

acrylic on canvas,stitch

20 pieces, each 73 x 61cm

Creation

2004

video; recorded sounds of

sewing and foetal heart-beat;

music for foetus

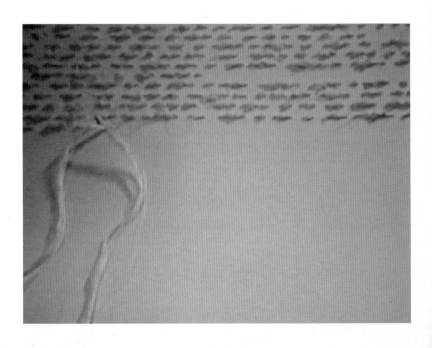

I wish to communicate God's message to man, and man's response,

in forms which are at once abstract and concrete, complex and simple.

Born 1970, Seoul

Education and Awards

1992 Excellence Prize, Korean Textile Design Exhibition, Koex Centre, Seoul

Grand Prize, Hong-ik Fiber Plastic Arts, Seoul Art Centre, Seoul

1996 MFA Hong-ik University, Seoul

Selected Exhibitions

2005 Yokohama International Art Fair, Yokohama City Art Centre, Japan (solo)

'Namnam Bukyeu' Exhibition, Gana Art Centre, Seoul

2004 'Message & Code', Gallery Biim, Seoul (solo)

International Contemporary Textile Art Exhibition, Daegu Exco, Daegu

2003 'Text' Exhibition, Art Space Hue, Seoul

'Korea & Japan', Basketry Exhibition, Silk Gallery, Seoul

International Textilkunst Graz, Austria

2002 'Time, Space, and Light', Sungbo Gallery, Seoul (solo)

'Object & Object', Duru Gallery, Seoul

2001 International Textile Symposium and Workshop, Graz, Austria

Nac-Yoem Hue Exhibition (China, Korea, Japan), Nagoya, Japan

Dream of Textile, Hansan Ramie Hall, Hansan

Hong-ik Fiber & Plastic Art Exhibition, Seoul Museum of Art, Seoul

2000 Ornament of Straw and Glass, Museum of Straw Arts, Seoul

The Grand Craft Exhibition, Iksan Cultural Centre, Iksan

1999 Poems Written in Fabric, Mokkumto Gallery, Seoul

1998 Miniature Exhibition, Kwanhoon Gallery, Seoul

1997 Invited '97 Let's Focus on These Artists, Dong-A Gallery, Seoul

1996 Tapestry Group Exhibition with Young Artists, Munwhaeilbo Gallery, Seoul

Professional

Currently Lecturer at Hong-ik University and Khun-Kok University

opposite:

Light in Darkness

2002

paper

340 pieces, each 32 x 40cm

Korea volume 2

October 2006 | ISBN 1 902015 09 6 | Edited by Mi-Kyoung Lee

Featuring 10 artists, including:

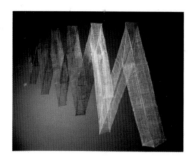

Chang-Yeon Soon

Kwang-Bin Park

Hwa-Jin Oh

Soonran Youn

Bora Kim

VOLUMES IN PREPARATION

Canada volume 1 ISBN 1 902015 15 0

Australia volume 2 ISBN 1 902015 14 2

Great Britain volume 3 ISBN 1 902015 16 9

뉴욕한국문화원
Korean Cultural Service NY